Cook it tonight!

Cup Cakes, Muffins & Brownies

COLLINS & BROWN

Recipes

Blueberry Muffins

Shopping list

- 2 medium eggs
- 250ml (9fl oz) semi-skimmed milk
- 250g (9oz) golden granulated sugar
- 2 tsp vanilla extract

Makes 12

Preparation Time
10 minutes

Cooking Time
20–25 minutes, plus cooling

- 350g (12oz) plain flour
- 4 tsp baking powder
- 250g (9oz) blueberries, frozen
- finely grated zest of 2 lemons

How to cook

1. Preheat the oven to 200°C (180°C fan oven) mark 6. Line a bun tin or muffin pan with 12 paper muffin cases.
2. Put the eggs, milk, sugar and vanilla extract into a bowl and mix well.
3. In another bowl, sift the flour and baking powder together, then add the blueberries and lemon zest. Toss together and then make a well in the centre.
4. Pour the egg mixture into the flour and blueberries, and mix in gently – overbeating will make the muffins tough.
5. Divide the mixture among the muffin cases and bake for 20–25 minutes. These are best eaten on the day they are made.

Vanilla Cup Cakes

Shopping list

- 125g (4oz) softened butter
- 125g (4oz) golden caster sugar
- 2 eggs

Makes 12

Preparation Time
15 minutes

Cooking Time
20 minutes

- [ ] 125g (4oz) self-raising flour
- [ ] 1 tbsp vanilla extract
- [ ] 200g (7oz) white chocolate

How to cook

1 Preheat the oven to 190°C (170°C fan oven) mark 5. Line a bun tin or muffin pan with 12 paper cases.

2 Beat the butter, sugar, eggs, flour and vanilla until smooth and creamy. Half-fill the muffin cases with the mixture and bake for 15–20 minutes until pale golden, risen and springy to the touch. Transfer to a wire rack to cool.

3 When the cupcakes are cool, melt the chocolate in a heatproof bowl set over a pan of gently simmering water. Stir until smooth and leave to cool slightly. Spoon the chocolate over the cakes and leave to set.

Cherry & Almond Muffins

Shopping list

- 225g (8oz) plain flour
- 1 tsp baking powder
- a pinch of salt
- 75g (3oz) caster sugar
- 50g (2oz) ground almonds

Makes 12

Preparation Time
10 minutes

Cooking Time
25 minutes, plus cooling

- 350g (12oz) glacé cherries, chopped
- 300ml (½ pint) milk
- 3 tbsp lemon juice
- 50ml (2fl oz) sunflower oil or melted butter
- 1 large egg
- 1 tsp almond extract
- roughly crushed sugar cubes to decorate

How to cook

1. Preheat the oven to 190°C (170°C fan oven) mark 5. Line a bun tin with 12 paper muffin cases.

2. Sift together the flour, baking powder and salt. Add the caster sugar and ground almonds. Stir in the chopped cherries.

3. Whisk together the milk, lemon juice, oil or butter, the egg and almond extract. Pour into the dry ingredients and stir tuntil all the ingredients are just combined – the mixture should be lumpy. Do not overmix or the muffins will be tough.

4. Spoon the mixture into the muffin cases. Sprinkle with the crushed sugar cubes and bake for about 25 minutes until well risen and golden.

5. Leave the muffins to cool in the tin for 5 minutes, then transfer to a wire rack to cool completely. These muffins are best eaten on the day they are made.

Double-chocolate Brownies

Shopping list

- 250g (9oz) butter, plus extra to grease
- 250g (9oz) plain chocolate (at least 50% cocoa solids), broken into pieces
- 100g (3½oz) white chocolate, broken into pieces

Makes 16

Preparation Time
15 minutes

Cooking Time
20–25 minutes, plus cooling

- 4 medium eggs
- 175g (6oz) light muscovado sugar
- 1 tsp vanilla extract
- 75g (3oz) plain flour, sifted
- 1/4 tsp baking powder
- 1 tbsp cocoa powder, sifted, plus extra to dust
- 100g (3 1/2oz) pecan nuts, chopped
- a pinch of salt
- a little icing sugar to dust

How to cook

1 Preheat the oven to 200°C (180°C fan oven) mark 6. Grease and baseline a 20.5cm (8in) square shallow tin. Melt the butter and plain chocolate in a heatproof bowl over a pan of gently simmering water. Remove the bowl from the pan and put to one side.

2 In a separate bowl, melt the white chocolate over a pan of gently simmering water. Put to one side.

3 Put the eggs into a separate large bowl. Add the muscovado sugar and vanilla extract, and whisk together until the mixture is pale and thick.

4 Add the flour, baking powder, cocoa powder, pecan nuts and salt to the bowl, then carefully pour in the dark chocolate mixture. Fold the ingredients together using a large metal spoon to make a smooth batter.

5 Pour the mixture into the tin. Spoon dollops of the white chocolate over the brownie mix, then swirl a skewer through it to create a marbled effect. Bake for 20–25 minutes. The brownies should still be fudgy inside and cracked and crispy on top.

6 Leave to cool in the tin. Transfer the brownies to a board and cut into 16 pieces. Dust with a little icing sugar and cocoa powder.

White Chocolate Vanilla Cup Cakes

Shopping list

- 125g (4oz) unsalted butter, at room temperature
- 125g (4oz) golden caster sugar
- 1 vanilla pod
- 2 medium eggs

Makes 12

Preparation Time
25 minutes

Cooking Time
15–20 minutes, plus cooling

- 125g (4oz) self-raising flour, sifted
- 1 tbsp vanilla extract
- 200g (7oz) white chocolate, in small pieces

For the frosted flowers

- 1 medium egg white
- 6 edible violets
- caster sugar to dust

How to cook

1 Preheat the oven to 190°C (170°C fan oven) mark 5. Line a bun tin with 12 paper muffin cases.

2 Put the butter and sugar in a bowl. Split the vanilla pod lengthways, scrape out the seeds and add to the bowl. Add the eggs, flour and vanilla extract, and beat thoroughly, using an electric whisk, until smooth and creamy. Spoon the mixture into the muffin cases and bake for 15–20 minutes until pale golden, risen and springy to the touch. Leave in the tin for 2–3 minutes, then transfer to a wire rack to cool.

3 To make the frosted flowers, whisk the egg white in a clean bowl for 30 seconds until frothy. Brush over the violet petals and put on a wire rack. Lightly dust with caster sugar and leave to dry.

4 Melt the chocolate in a heatproof bowl set over a pan of gently simmering water. Stir until smooth and leave to cool slightly. Spoon the chocolate on to the cakes, top with a frosted flower and leave to set.

Cherry Chip Cookies

Shopping list

- 75g (3oz) unsalted butter, softened, plus extra to grease
- 25g (1oz) caster sugar
- 50g (2oz) light soft brown sugar
- a few drops of vanilla extract

Makes 14

Preparation Time
20 minutes

Cooking Time
10–12 minutes, plus cooling

- 1 large egg, lightly beaten
- 175g (6oz) self-raising flour, sifted
- finely grated zest of 1 orange
- 125g (4oz) white chocolate, roughly broken
- 125g (4oz) glacé cherries, roughly chopped
- icing sugar to dust

How to cook

1 Preheat the oven to 180°C (160°C fan oven) mark 4 and grease two baking sheets. Beat together the butter, caster sugar, light brown sugar and vanilla extract until well combined, using an electric whisk. Gradually beat in the egg until the mixture is light and fluffy.

2 With a metal spoon, lightly fold in the flour, orange zest, chocolate and glacé cherries. Put tablespoonfuls of the mixture on to the prepared baking sheets and bake for 10–12 minutes. The biscuits should be soft under a crisp crust.

3 Leave the cookies on the baking sheet for 1 minute, then transfer to a wire rack to cool completely. Store in an airtight container for up to three days. Dust with icing sugar just before serving.

Brown Sugar Muffins

Shopping list

- 12 brown sugar cubes
- 150g (5oz) plain flour
- 1 1/2 tsp baking powder
- 1/4 tsp salt
- 1 medium egg, beaten

Makes 6

Preparation Time
10 minutes

Cooking Time
30–35 minutes, plus cooling

- 40g (1 1/2oz) golden caster sugar
- 50g (2oz) unsalted butter, melted
- 1/2 tsp vanilla extract
- 100ml (3 1/2fl oz) milk

How to cook

1 Preheat the oven to 200°C (180°C fan oven) mark 6. Line a bun tin or muffin pan with six paper muffin cases.

2 Roughly crush the sugar cubes and put to one side. Sift together the flour, baking powder and salt.

3 In a large bowl, combine the beaten egg, caster sugar, melted butter, vanilla extract and milk.

4 Fold in the sifted flour and spoon the mixture into the muffin cases. Sprinkle with the brown sugar. Bake for 30–35 minutes. Cool on a wire rack.

Chocolate Banana Muffins

Shopping list

- 275g (10oz) self-raising flour
- 1 tsp bicarbonate of soda
- 1/2 tsp salt
- 3 large bananas, about 450g (1lb)
- 125g (4oz) golden caster sugar

Makes 12

Preparation Time
15 minutes

Cooking Time
20 minutes, plus cooling

- 1 large egg, beaten
- 50ml (2fl oz) semi-skimmed milk
- 75g (3oz) unsalted butter, melted and cooled
- 50g (2oz) plain chocolate, chopped

How to cook

1 Preheat the oven to 180°C (160°C fan oven) mark 4. Line a bun tin or muffin pan with 12 paper muffin cases. Sift the flour, bicarbonate of soda and salt together into a large mixing bowl and put to one side.

2 Peel the bananas and mash with a fork in a bowl. Add the caster sugar, egg, milk and melted butter, and mix until well combined.

3 Add this to the flour mixture, with the chopped chocolate. Stir gently, using only a few strokes, until the flour is only just incorporated – do not overmix. The mixture should be lumpy.

4 Spoon the mixture into the muffin cases, half-filling them. Bake in the oven for 20 minutes or until the muffins are well risen and golden. Transfer to a wire rack to cool. Serve warm or cold.

Red Nose Buns

Shopping list

- 50g (2oz) very soft butter
- 50g (2oz) caster sugar
- 1 medium egg, beaten
- 50g (2oz) self-raising flour
- 1/4 tsp baking powder

Makes 36

Preparation Time
20 minutes

Cooking Time
12–15 minutes, plus cooling

- 1 ripe banana, peeled and mashed
- 125g (4oz) icing sugar, sifted
- about 1 tbsp orange juice
- red glacé cherries or round red jelly sweets to decorate

How to cook

1. Preheat the oven to 190°C (170°C fan oven) mark 5. Put the butter, caster sugar, egg, flour and baking powder in a food processor and process until smooth and well mixed. Add the banana and process for 1 minute.

2. Arrange about 36 petits fours cases on baking sheets. Put a teaspoonful of the mixture into each case. Bake for about 12–15 minutes until golden. Transfer to a wire rack to cool.

3. When the buns are cold, make glacé icing by mixing the icing sugar with the orange juice until smooth and just thick enough to coat the back of a spoon. Top each bun with a small blob of icing and stick half a cherry or a sweet on each one. Leave to set.

Macaroons

Shopping list

- 2 medium egg whites
- 125g (4oz) caster sugar
- 125g (4oz) ground almonds
- ¼ tsp almond extract
- 22 blanched almonds

Makes 22

Preparation Time
10 minutes

Cooking Time
12–15 minutes, plus cooling

How to cook

1 Preheat the oven to 180°C (160°C fan oven) mark 4 and line two baking sheets with baking parchment. In a large bowl, whisk the egg whites until they form stiff peaks. Gradually fold in the sugar, then gently stir in the almonds and almond extract.

2 Spoon teaspoonfuls of the mixture on to the baking sheets, spacing them slightly apart. Press an almond into each and bake for 12–15 minutes until just golden and firm to the touch.

3 Leave on the baking sheets for 10 minutes, then transfer to a wire rack to cool completely. Store in an airtight container for up to one week.

Cherry Chocolate Fudge Brownies

Shopping list

- 150g (5oz) unsalted butter, plus extra to grease
- 200g (7oz) plain chocolate (70% cocoa solids)
- 175g (6oz) caster sugar
- 2 tsp vanilla extract

Makes 12

Preparation Time
20 minutes

Cooking Time
50 minutes,
plus cooling and
1 hour setting

- 5 medium eggs
- 1175g (6oz) plain flour
- 3/4 tsp baking powder
- 250g (9oz) glacé cherries, halved

For the icing

- 150g (5oz) plain chocolate (70% cocoa solids)
- 2 tbsp Kirsch
- 4 tbsp double cream

How to cook

1 Preheat the oven to 180°C (160°C fan oven) mark 4. Grease and baseline an 18cm (7in) square shallow cake tin. Put the butter and chocolate in a heatproof bowl over a pan of gently simmering water. Leave the chocolate to melt without stirring. Remove the bowl from the pan and stir until smooth. Leave to cool.

2 In a bowl, whisk the sugar, vanilla extract and eggs until pale and thick. Stir the chocolate into the egg mixture. Sift the flour and baking powder together and lightly fold into the mixture with the cherries. Pour the mixture into the prepared tin. Bake for 40 minutes or until just set. Cool slightly in the tin before icing.

3 To make the icing, put the chocolate and Kirsch in a heatproof bowl over a pan of gently simmering water. Once melted, add the cream and 4 tbsp water, and stir well. Pour over the brownie and leave to set. Cut into 12 squares.

Chocolate Cup Cakes

Shopping list

- 125g (4oz) unsalted butter, softened
- 125g (4oz) light muscovado sugar
- 2 medium eggs, beaten
- 15g (1/2oz) cocoa powder

Makes 18

Preparation Time
15 minutes

Cooking Time
20 minutes, plus cooling and setting

- 100g (3½oz) self-raising flour
- 100g (3½oz) plain chocolate (at least 70% cocoa solids), roughly chopped

For the topping

- 150ml (¼ pint) double cream
- 100g (3½oz) plain chocolate (at least 70% cocoa solids), broken up

How to cook

1. Preheat the oven to 190°C (170°C fan oven) mark 5. Line bun tins or muffin pans with 18 paper muffin cases.

2. Beat together the butter and sugar until light and fluffy. Gradually beat in the eggs. Sift the cocoa powder with the flour and fold into the creamed mixture with the chopped chocolate.

3. Divide the mixture among the paper cases and lightly flatten the surface with the back of a spoon. Bake for 20 minutes. Cool in the cases.

4. For the topping, put the cream and broken-up chocolate into a heavy-based pan over a low heat and heat until melted, then allow to cool and thicken slightly. Pour over the cooled cakes and leave to set for 30 minutes.

Dainty Cup Cakes

Shopping list

- 175g (6oz) unsalted butter, softened
- 175g (6oz) golden caster sugar
- 3 medium eggs
- 175g (6oz) self-raising flour, sifted
- finely grated zest and juice of 1 lemon

Makes 12

Preparation Time
15 minutes

Cooking Time
15–20 minutes, plus cooling

For the frosted flowers

- 1 medium egg white
- 6 edible flowers, such as violas
- caster sugar to dust

For the icing

- 225g (8oz) icing sugar, sifted
- 1 drop violet food colouring
- 2–3 tbsp lemon juice, strained

How to cook

1 Preheat the oven to 190°C (170°C fan oven) mark 5. Line a bun tin or muffin pan with 12 paper muffin cases.

2 Put the butter and caster sugar in a bowl and cream together until pale, light and fluffy. Add the eggs, one at a time, and beat together, folding 1 tbsp flour into the mixture if it looks as if it is going to curdle. Fold in the flour, lemon zest and juice, and mix everything well.

3 Spoon the mixture into the cases and bake for 15–20 minutes until pale golden, risen and springy to the touch. Cool on a wire rack.

4 To make the frosted flowers, whisk the egg white in a clean bowl for 30 seconds until frothy. Brush over the flower petals and put on a wire rack resting on a piece of greaseproof paper. Dust heavily with caster sugar, then leave the flowers to dry.

5 To make the icing, put the icing sugar into a bowl with the violet food colouring. Mix in the lemon juice to make a smooth dropping consistency. Spoon the icing on to the cakes. Decorate with the frosted flowers and leave until the icing is set.

Wholemeal Banana Muffins

Shopping list

- butter to grease (optional)
- 50g (2oz) raisins
- finely grated zest and juice of 1 orange
- 125g (4oz) wholemeal flour
- 25g (1oz) wheatgerm
- 3 tbsp caster sugar

Makes 6

Preparation Time
15 minutes, plus 1 hour soaking

Cooking Time
20–25 minutes

- 2 tsp baking powder
- a pinch of salt
- 1 large medium egg, beaten
- 50ml (2fl oz) milk
- 50ml (2fl oz) sunflower oil
- 2 medium-sized bananas, mashed

For the topping

- 5 tbsp orange marmalade
- 50g (2oz) banana chips, roughly chopped
- 50g (2oz) walnuts, roughly chopped

How to cook

1 Preheat the oven to 200℃ (180℃ fan oven) mark 6. Line a bun tin or muffin pan with six paper muffin cases. Put the raisins in a bowl, pour the orange juice over and leave to soak for 1 hour.

2 Put the orange zest in a bowl with the flour, wheatgerm, sugar, baking powder and salt, and mix together. Make a well in the centre.

3 In a separate bowl, mix the egg, milk and oil, then pour into the flour mixture and stir until just blended. Drain the raisins, reserving 1 tbsp juice, and stir into the mixture with the bananas. Don' t overmix. Fill each muffin case two-thirds full. Bake for 20–25 minutes until a skewer inserted into the centre comes out clean. Transfer to a wire rack to cool slightly.

4 For the topping, gently heat the marmalade with the reserved orange juice until melted. Simmer for 1 minute, then add the banana chips and walnuts. Spoon on top of the muffins. Serve while still warm.

Almond Cookies

Shopping list

- rice paper to line
- 2 medium egg whites
- 200g (7oz) caster sugar
- 200g (7oz) ground almonds
- finely grated zest of 1 orange

Makes 12

Preparation Time
15 minutes

Cooking Time
15–20 minutes, plus cooling

- $^1/_2$ tsp ground ginger
- 40g ($1^1/_2$oz) stem ginger in syrup, drained and roughly chopped
- 2 tbsp plain flour, sifted, to dust
- 12 natural glacé cherries

How to cook

1. Preheat the oven to 180°C (160°C fan oven) mark 4. Line two baking sheets with rice paper. Put the egg whites in a large bowl and whisk until they form stiff peaks. In another large bowl, stir together the sugar, ground almonds, orange zest, $^1/_4$ tsp ground ginger and the stem ginger. With a wooden spoon, mix in the egg whites to form a sticky dough.

2. Roll the dough into 12 equal-sized balls. Mix together the flour and the remaining ground ginger in a bowl. Lightly coat each ball in the flour and shake off the excess. Put the balls, spaced well apart, on to the prepared baking sheets.

3. Flatten each ball into a round. Push a glacé cherry in the middle of each cookie and bake for 15–20 minutes until lightly golden.

4. Cool on a wire rack, then trim away the excess rice paper. Store in an airtight container for up to one week.

Low-fat Brownies

Shopping list

- 50ml (2fl oz) sunflower oil, plus extra to grease
- 250g (9oz) plain chocolate (at least 50% cocoa solids)
- 4 medium eggs

Makes 16

Preparation Time
10 minutes

Cooking Time
20 minutes, plus cooling

- 150g (5oz) light muscovado sugar
- 1 tsp vanilla extract
- 75g (3oz) plain flour
- 1/4 tsp baking powder
- 1 tbsp cocoa powder

How to cook

1. Preheat the oven to 200°C (180°C fan oven) mark 6. Grease and line a 20.5cm (8in) square shallow tin.

2. Melt the chocolate in a heatproof bowl over a pan of gently simmering water. Remove the bowl from the pan and put to one side to cool slightly.

3. Put the eggs into a large bowl, add the sunflower oil, sugar and vanilla extract, and whisk together until pale and thick. Sift the flour, baking powder and cocoa powder into the bowl, then carefully pour in the chocolate. Using a large metal spoon, gently fold all the ingredients together – if you fold too roughly, the chocolate will seize up and become unusable.

4. Carefully pour the brownie mixture into the prepared tin and bake for 20 minutes – when cooked, the brownies should still be fudgy in the centre and the top should be cracked and crispy. Cut into 16 squares immediately, then leave to cool in the tin. To store, wrap in clingfilm and store in an airtight container for up to three days.

Sour Cherry Cakes

Shopping list

- 175g (6oz) unsalted butter, softened
- 175g (6oz) golden caster sugar
- 3 medium eggs
- 175g (6oz) self-raising flour, sifted

Makes 12

Preparation Time
30 minutes

Cooking Time
15–20 minutes, plus cooling

- 75g (3oz) dried cherries
- 2 tbsp milk
- 225g (8oz) golden icing sugar, sifted
- 3 tbsp lemon juice, strained

How to cook

1. Preheat the oven to 190°C (170°C fan oven) mark 5. Line a bun tin or muffin pan with 12 paper muffin cases.

2. Put the butter and caster sugar in a bowl and cream together until pale, light and fluffy. Beat in the eggs, one at a time, folding in 1 tbsp flour if the mixture looks like it is starting to curdle.

3. Put 12 dried cherries to one side. Fold the remaining flour, cherries and the milk into the creamed mixture until evenly combined. Spoon the mixture into the paper cases and bake for 15–20 minutes until pale golden and risen. Remove from the tin and cool on a wire rack.

4. Put the icing sugar in a bowl and mix with the lemon juice to make a smooth dropping consistency. Spoon on to the cakes and decorate each with a cherry.

Spiced Star Biscuits

Shopping list

- 2 tbsp runny honey
- 25g (1oz) unsalted butter
- 50g (2oz) light muscovado sugar
- finely grated zest of 1/2 lemon
- finely grated zest of 1/2 orange
- 225g (8oz) self-raising flour, plus extra to roll out

Makes 35

Preparation Time
15 minutes, plus
4 hours chilling

Cooking Time
15–20 minutes,
plus cooling

- 1 tsp ground cinnamon
- 1 tsp ground ginger
- ½ tsp freshly grated nutmeg
- pinch of ground cloves
- a pinch of salt
- 1 tbsp finely chopped candied peel
- 50g (2oz) ground almonds
- 1 large egg, beaten
- 1½ tbsp milk

For the decoration

- 150g (5oz) icing sugar
- silver sugar balls

How to cook

1 Put the honey, butter, muscovado sugar and citrus zests into a small pan and stir over a low heat until the butter has melted and the ingredients are well combined.

2 Sift the flour, spices and salt together into a bowl, then add the chopped candied peel and ground almonds. Add the melted mixture, beaten egg and milk and mix until the dough comes together. Knead the dough briefly until smooth, then wrap in clingfilm and chill for at least 4 hours, or overnight.

3 Preheat the oven to 180°C (160°C fan oven) mark 4. Roll out the dough on a floured surface to 5mm (¼ in) thick. Using a 5cm (2in) cutter, stamp out stars and put on to baking sheets. Bake for 15–20 minutes or until just beginning to brown at the edges.

4 Transfer the biscuits to a wire rack to cool. To decorate, mix the icing sugar with 1½ tbsp warm water making a smooth icing. Coat some of the biscuits with icing and finish with a piped edging if you like, then decorate with silver balls. Pipe dots of icing on the plain biscuits and attach silver balls. Allow the icing to set, then store the biscuits in an airtight container for up to one week.

The Ultimate Chocolate Brownie

Shopping list

- 200g (7oz) butter, plus extra to grease
- 400g (14oz) plain chocolate
- 225g (8oz) light muscovado sugar
- 1 tsp vanilla extract
- 150g (5oz) pecan nuts, roughly chopped

Makes 16

Preparation Time
15 minutes

Cooking Time
1 hour 20 minutes, plus 2 hours cooling

- 25g (1oz) cocoa powder, sifted, plus extra to dust (optional)
- 75g (3oz) self-raising flour, sifted
- 3 large eggs, beaten

How to cook

1. Preheat the oven to 170℃ (150℃ fan oven) mark 3. Grease a 20.5cm (8in) square shallow cake tin and line the base with non-stick baking parchment. Put the butter and chocolate in a heatproof bowl over a pan of gently simmering water and stir until melted. Remove from the heat and stir in the sugar, vanilla extract, pecan nuts, cocoa, flour and eggs.
2. Turn the mixture into the prepared tin and level the surface with the back of a spoon. Bake for about 1 hour 15 minutes or until set on the surface but still soft underneath.
3. Leave to cool in the tin for 2 hours. Turn out, dust with sifted cocoa powder, if using, and cut into squares. Eat cold or serve warm with ice cream.

Spiced Carrot Muffins

Shopping list

- 125g (4oz) unsalted butter, softened
- 125g (4oz) light muscovado sugar
- 3 pieces of preserved stem ginger, chopped
- 150g (5oz) self-raising flour, sifted
- 1½ tsp baking powder
- 1 tbsp ground mixed spice
- 25g (1oz) ground almonds

Makes 12

Preparation Time
30 minutes

Cooking Time
20–25 minutes, plus cooling

- 3 medium eggs
- finely grated zest of 1/2 orange
- 150g (5oz) carrots, grated
- 50g (2oz) pecan nuts, chopped
- 50g (2oz) sultanas
- 3 tbsp white rum or orange liqueur (optional)

For the icing

- 200g (7oz) full-fat cream cheese
- 75g (3oz) icing sugar
- 1 tsp lemon juice
- 12 unsprayed rose petals to decorate (optional)

How to cook

1 Preheat the oven to 180°C (160°C fan oven) mark 4. Line a bun tin or muffin pan with 12 paper muffin cases.

2 Beat together the butter, muscovado sugar and stem ginger until pale and creamy.

3 Add the flour, baking powder, spice, ground almonds, eggs and orange zest. Beat well until combined.

4 Stir in the carrots, pecan nuts and sultanas. Divide the mixture among the muffin cases and bake for about 20–25 minutes until risen and just firm. A skewer inserted into the centre should come out clean. Transfer to a wire rack and leave to cool.

5 To make the icing, beat the cream cheese in a bowl until softened. Beat in the icing sugar and lemon juice to give a smooth icing that just holds its shape.

6 Drizzle each cake with a little liqueur, if using. Use a small palette knife to spread a little icing over each cake. Decorate each with a petal, if you like.

Chocolate Butterfly Cakes

Shopping list

- 125g (4oz) butter, very soft
- 125g (4oz) caster sugar
- 2 medium eggs, lightly beaten individually

Makes 18

Preparation Time
25 minutes

Cooking Time
15–20 minutes, plus cooling

- 125g (4oz) plain flour
- 25g (1oz) cocoa
- ½ tsp baking powder
- 1 tbsp milk

For the buttercream

- 75g (3oz) unsalted butter
- 175g (6oz) icing sugar, sifted
- a few drops of vanilla extract
- 1–2 tbsp milk

How to cook

1. Preheat the oven to 190°C (170°C fan oven) mark 5. Put 18 paper cake cases into two bun trays. With an electric hand whisk, beat the butter and sugar together until soft and fluffy and lighter in colour. Beat in the eggs thoroughly, one at a time.

2. Sift the flour, cocoa and baking powder into the bowl and fold in gently until well mixed. Fold in the milk to give a soft, dropping consistency.

3. Divide the mixture between the cases and bake for 15–20 minutes until firm. Cool on a wire rack.

4. To make the buttercream, soften the butter in a mixing bowl, then beat until light and fluffy. Gradually stir in the remaining ingredients and beat until smooth. Allow the icing to settle before using.

5. Slice off the top of each cake and cut the slice in half. Spread buttercream on each cake with a palette knife. Put the butterfly wings on top, with their curved sides facing away from each other.

Sultana & Pecan Cookies

Shopping list

- 225g (8oz) unsalted butter, at room temperature, plus extra to grease
- 175g (6oz) light muscovado sugar
- 2 medium eggs, lightly beaten
- 225g (8oz) pecan nut halves

Makes 20

Preparation Time
15 minutes

Cooking Time
12–15 minutes, plus cooling

- 300g (11oz) self-raising flour, sifted
- ¼ tsp baking powder
- 125g (4oz) sultanas
- 2 tbsp maple syrup

How to cook

1. Preheat the oven to 190°C (170°C fan oven) mark 5 and grease four baking sheets.
2. Cream together the butter and sugar until the mixture is pale and fluffy. Gradually beat in the eggs until thoroughly combined.
3. Put 20 pecan nut halves to one side, then roughly chop the rest and fold into the mixture with the flour, baking powder, sultanas and maple syrup.
4. Roll the mixture into 20 balls and place them, spaced well apart, on the baking sheets. Flatten the cookies with a dampened palette knife and top each with a piece of pecan nut. Bake for 12–15 minutes until pale golden.
5. Leave on the baking sheets for 5 minutes, then transfer to a wire rack to cool completely.

Wheat-free Blueberry Muffins

Shopping list

- 250g (9oz) wheat-free flour
- 2 tsp wheat-free baking powder
- 1 tsp bicarbonate of soda
- 125g (4oz) golden caster sugar
- 75g (3oz) ground almonds
- finely grated zest of 1 lemon

Makes 12

Preparation Time
15 minutes

Cooking Time
15 minutes

- 125g (4oz) dried blueberries
- 1 medium egg
- 1 tsp vanilla extract
- 250ml (9fl oz) skimmed milk
- 50g (2oz) unsalted butter, melted

How to cook

1 Preheat the oven to 200°C (180°C fan oven) mark 6. Line a muffin tin with 12 paper muffin cases.

2 Put the flour, baking powder and bicarbonate of soda into a bowl, then stir in the caster sugar, ground almonds, lemon zest and dried blueberries.

3 Put the egg, vanilla extract, milk and butter into a jug and mix together with a fork. Pour this liquid into the dry ingredients and lightly fold together.

4 Spoon the mixture into the muffin cases to three-quarters fill them and bake in the oven for 15 minutes or until the muffins are risen, pale golden and just firm.

5 Transfer the muffins to a wire rack and leave to cool slightly before serving.

Kitten Cup Cakes

Shopping list

- 125g (4oz) butter, very soft
- 125g (4oz) caster sugar
- grated zest of 1 lemon
- 2 medium eggs, beaten
- 125g (4oz) self-raising flour, sifted

Makes 12

Preparation Time
25 minutes

Cooking Time
20 minutes, plus cooling

For the decoration

- 175g (6oz) icing sugar
- black and assorted writing icings
- jelly diamonds and Smarties
- black liquorice laces, cut into short lengths

How to cook

1 Preheat the oven to 190°C (170°C fan oven) mark 5. Put paper cases in a 12-hole bun tin.

2 Beat the butter, caster sugar and lemon zest together with an electric hand whisk until pale and fluffy. Add the eggs, a little at a time, beating well after each addition. Fold in the flour. Divide the mixture between the paper cases. Bake for about 20 minutes until golden and risen. Cool on a wire rack.

3 Sift the icing sugar into a bowl. Stir in 1–2 tbsp warm water, a few drops at a time, until you have a smooth, spreadable icing. Slice the tops off the cooled buns to make them level, if necessary. Cover the top of each cake with icing.

4 Decorate the buns to make kittens faces. Use black writing icing for the eyes, halve the jelly diamonds for the ears, press a Smartie in the centre for a nose, and use black writing icing to draw on a mouth. Use different coloured writing icing for the pupils and markings. Stick on liquorice whiskers.

Peanut & Raisin Cookies

Shopping list

- 125g (4oz) unsalted butter, softened, plus extra to grease
- 150g (5oz) caster sugar
- 1 medium egg
- 150g (5oz) plain flour, sifted

Makes 30

Preparation Time
10 minutes

Cooking Time
15 minutes, plus cooling

- 1/2 tsp baking powder
- 1/2 tsp salt
- 125g (4oz) crunchy peanut butter
- 175g (6oz) raisins

How to cook

1. Preheat the oven to 190°C (170°C fan oven) mark 5 and grease two baking sheets. Beat together all the ingredients except the raisins, until well blended. Stir in the raisins.

2. Spoon large teaspoonfuls of the mixture on to the baking sheets, leaving room for the mixture to spread. Bake for about 15 minutes or until golden brown around the edges.

3. Leave to cool slightly, then transfer to a wire rack to cool completely.

Chocolate Fudge Brownies

Shopping list

- butter to grease
- 125g (4oz) milk chocolate
- 9 ready-to-eat prunes
- 200g (7oz) light muscovado sugar
- 3 large egg whites

Makes 12

Preparation Time
20 minutes

Cooking Time
1 hour, plus cooling

- 1 tsp vanilla extract
- 75g (3oz) plain flour, sifted
- 50g (2oz) white chocolate, chopped
- icing sugar to dust

How to cook

1 Preheat the oven to 180°C (160°C fan oven) mark 4. Grease and baseline a 15cm (6in) square shallow cake tin. Melt the milk chocolate in a heatproof bowl over a pan of gently simmering water. Remove from the heat and leave to cool slightly.

2 Put the prunes in a food processor or blender with 100ml (3½fl oz) water and whiz for 2–3 minutes to make a purée. Add the muscovado sugar and whiz briefly to mix.

3 In a clean, grease-free bowl, whisk the egg whites until they form soft peaks.

4 Add the vanilla extract, prune mixture, flour, white chocolate and egg whites to the bowl of melted chocolate. Fold everything together gently. Pour the mixture into the prepared tin and bake for 1 hour or until firm to the touch.

5 Leave to cool in the tin. Turn out, dust with icing sugar and cut into 12 squares.

Bran & Apple Muffins

Shopping list

- 250ml (9fl oz) semi-skimmed milk
- 2 tbsp orange juice
- 50g (2oz) All Bran
- 9 ready-to-eat prunes
- 100g ($3\frac{1}{2}$oz) light muscovado sugar
- 2 medium egg whites

Makes 10

Preparation Time
20 minutes

Cooking Time
30 minutes

- 1 tbsp golden syrup
- 150g (5oz) plain flour, sifted
- 1 tsp baking powder
- 1 tsp ground cinnamon
- 1 eating apple, peeled and grated
- demerara sugar to sprinkle

How to cook

1 Preheat the oven to 190°C (170°C fan oven) mark 5. Line a bun tin or muffin pan with ten paper muffin cases.

2 In a bowl, mix the milk and orange juice with the All Bran. Put to one side for 10 minutes.

3 Put the prunes in a food processor or blender with 100ml (3½fl oz) water and whiz for 2–3 minutes to make a purée, then add the muscovado sugar and whiz briefly to mix.

4 In a grease-free bowl, whisk the egg whites until they form soft peaks, Add the whites to the milk mixture with the golden syrup, flour, baking powder, cinnamon, grated apple and prune mixture. Fold all the ingredients together gently.

5 Spoon the mixture into the muffin cases and bake for 30 minutes or until well risen and golden brown. Sprinkle with demerara sugar just before serving.

Fairy Cakes

Shopping list

- 125g (4oz) self-raising flour, sifted
- 1 tsp baking powder
- 125g (4oz) caster sugar
- 125g (4oz) butter, very soft
- 2 medium eggs

Makes 18

Preparation Time
20 minutes

Cooking Time
10–15 minutes, plus cooling

- 1 tbsp milk
- 225g (8oz) icing sugar, sifted
- assorted food colourings (optional)
- sweets, sprinkles or coloured sugar to decorate

How to cook

1. Preheat the oven to 200°C (180°C fan oven) mark 6. Put paper cases into 18 of the holes in two bun tins. Put the flour, baking powder, sugar, butter, eggs and milk in a mixing bowl and beat with an electric hand whisk for 2 minutes until the mixture is pale and very soft.

2. Half-fill each paper case with the mixture. Bake for 10–15 minutes until golden brown. Transfer to a wire rack to cool.

3. Put the icing sugar in a bowl and gradually blend in 2–3 tbsp warm water until the icing is fairly stiff, but spreadable. Add a couple of drops of food colouring, if you like. When the cakes are cold, spread the tops with the icing and decorate.

White Chocolate & Nut Brownies

Shopping list

- 75g (3oz) unsalted butter, plus extra to grease
- 500g (1lb 2oz) white chocolate, roughly chopped
- 3 large eggs
- 175g (6oz) golden caster sugar

Makes 12

Preparation Time
20 minutes

Cooking Time
30–35 minutes, plus cooling

- 175g (6oz) self-raising flour
- a pinch of salt
- 175g (6oz) macadamia nuts, roughly chopped
- 1 tsp vanilla extract

How to cook

1 Preheat the oven to 190°C (170°C fan oven) mark 5. Grease and line a 25.5 x 20.5cm (10 x 8in) baking tin.

2 Melt 125g (4oz) white chocolate with the butter in a heatproof bowl over a pan of gently simmering water, stirring occasionally. Remove the bowl from the pan and leave to cool slightly.

3 Whisk the eggs and sugar together in a large bowl until smooth, then gradually beat in the melted chocolate mixture; the consistency will become quite firm. Sift the flour and salt over the mixture, then fold in with the nuts, the remaining chopped chocolate and the vanilla extract.

4 Turn the mixture into the prepared tin and level the surface. Bake for 30–35 minutes until risen and golden and the centre is just firm to the touch – the mixture will still be soft under the crust; it firms up on cooling. Leave to cool in the tin. Turn out and cut into 12 squares. Store in an airtight container for up to one week.

White & Dark Chocolate Cookies

Shopping list

- 125g (4oz) unsalted butter, softened, plus extra to grease
- 125g (4oz) golden caster sugar
- 2 medium eggs, beaten
- 2 tsp vanilla extract
- 250g (9oz) self-raising flour, sifted

Makes 26

Preparation Time
15 minutes, plus 30 minutes chilling

Cooking Time
10–12 minutes, plus cooling

- finely grated zest of 1 orange
- 100g (3½oz) white chocolate, roughly chopped
- 100g (3½oz) plain chocolate (at least 70% cocoa solids), roughly chopped

How to cook

1. Preheat the oven to 180°C (160°C fan oven) mark 4 and grease three baking sheets.

2. Cream together the butter and sugar until the mixture is pale and fluffy. Gradually beat in the eggs and vanilla extract. Sift in the flour, add the orange zest then sprinkle in the white and dark chocolate. Mix the dough together with your hands. Knead lightly, then wrap in clingfilm. Chill the cookie mixture for at least 30 minutes.

3. Divide the mixture into 26 pieces and roll each into a ball. Flatten each ball slightly to make a disc, then put on to the prepared baking sheets, spaced well apart. Bake for about 10–12 minutes until golden.

4. Leave on the baking sheet for 5 minutes, then transfer to a wire rack to cool completely.

Other titles available:

First published in Great Britain in 2009
by Collins & Brown
10 Southcombe Street
London W14 0RA

An imprint of Anova Books Company Ltd
www.anovabooks.com

The Good Housekeeping website is:
www.allaboutyou.com/goodhousekeeping

ISBN 978-1-84340-558-0

The recipes in this book have been chosen from titles in the Good Housekeeping Easy to Make! series.

A catalogue record for this book is available from the British Library.

Reproduction by Dot Gradations Ltd, UK
Printed and bound by Graphicom, Italy

Photography by Nicki Dowey.